MIRROR POWER

Library of Congress Cataloging-in-Publication Data

Strom, Laura Layton.
  Mirror power / by Laura Layton Strom.
    p. cm. -- (Shockwave)
  Includes index.
  ISBN-10: 0-531-17588-X (lib. bdg.)
  ISBN-13: 978-0-531-17588-0 (lib. bdg.)
  ISBN-10: 0-531-18772-1 (pbk.)
  ISBN-13: 978-0-531-18772-2 (pbk.)

  1. Mirrors--Juvenile literature. 2. Reflection (Optics)--Juvenile literature.
I. Title. II. Series.

  TP867.S87 2008
  681'.428--dc22

2007012244

Published in 2008 by Children's Press, an imprint of Scholastic Inc.,
557 Broadway, New York, New York 10012
www.scholastic.com

SCHOLASTIC, CHILDREN'S PRESS, and associated logos are trademarks
and/or registered trademarks of Scholastic Inc.

08 09 10 11 12 13 14 15 16 17
10 9 8 7 6 5 4 3 2 1

Printed in China through Colorcraft Ltd., Hong Kong

Author: Laura Layton Strom
Educational Consultant: Ian Morrison
Editor: Lynette Evans
Designer: Steve Clarke
Illustrator: Marten Coombe (mirrors in history, pp. 18–19)
Photo Researcher: Jamshed Mistry

Photographs by: Big Stock Photo (clip badge, p. 31); **Getty Images** (p. 7; guitarist, pp. 12–13;
elongated reflection of boy, p. 17; broken mirror, p. 29); **Image courtesy of Themeaddicts Inc.**
(p. 30); **Jennifer and Brian Lupton** (teenagers, pp. 32–33); **Photolibrary** (security mirror, p. 15;
mirror reflection of girl, p. 17; p. 23; *Alice Through the Looking Glass* sculpture, p. 29);
Rigel Woida (Mars, p. 31); **Stock.Xchng** (p. 5; ambulance, p. 11; kaleidoscope pattern, p. 26);
StockXpert (microscope, p. 22; girl with stop sign, p. 24; mirror-glass building, p. 27); **Tranz:**
Camera Press (p. 28); Corbis (cover; p. 3; pp. 8–9; girl, pp. 10–11; baby, p. 13; mirror image
of truck, pp. 14–15; p. 21; operation, p. 22; p. 25; girl looking through kaleidoscope, p. 26;
The Mirrored Room, p. 27; broken mirror, p. 29; digital ID system, p. 31; Earth and Mars,
pp. 32–33)

All illustrations and other photographs © Weldon Owen Education Inc.

MIRROR POWER

Laura Layton Strom

children's press®

An imprint of Scholastic Inc.
NEW YORK • TORONTO • LONDON • AUCKLAND • SYDNEY
MEXICO CITY • NEW DELHI • HONG KONG
DANBURY, CONNECTICUT

CHECK THESE OUT!

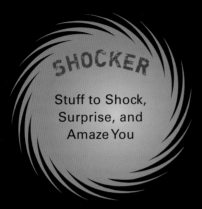

SHOCKER

Stuff to Shock,
Surprise, and
Amaze You

Quick Recaps
and Notable
Notes

Word Stunners
and Other Oddities

The Heads-Up
on Expert Reading

Links to More
Information

CONTENTS

HIGH-POWERED WORDS 6

GET ON THE WAVELENGTH 8

How Do Mirrors Work? 10

Plane Mirrors 12

Convex Mirrors 14

Concave Mirrors 16

Mirrors in History 18

Mirrors in Astronomy 20

Mirrors in Medicine 22

Mirrors for Light and Heat 24

Mirrors in Art and Design 26

Mirrors in Stories 28

Mirrors in the Future 30

AFTERSHOCKS 32

GLOSSARY 34

FIND OUT MORE 35

INDEX 36

ABOUT THE AUTHOR 36

absorb to soak up

concave curved inward, like the inside surface of a bowl

convex curved outward, like the outside of a ball

distort to make something crooked or out of shape

illusion (*i LOO zhuhn*) something that appears to exist but does not

magnify to make something appear larger

reflection (*rih FLEK shuhn*) an image seen on a shiny surface, such as a mirror, due to light bouncing off it

refract (*rih FRAKT*) to bend or slant a ray of light

- -

For additional vocabulary, see Glossary on page 34.

The word *concave* comes from the Latin *concavus*, meaning "hollow." The related word *cave* is defined as a natural hollow place.

A mirror makes it seem as if this girl is hovering in the air. In fact, she is standing on the ground.

Think about how many mirrors are in your home and in the world around you. Mirrors help you see yourself. They help you check for food in your teeth. They help a bus driver safely back up. They help people see what is coming around a corner. Mirrors help us see the moon through a telescope. Mirrors are even hidden inside ordinary objects, such as cameras.

An **image** in a mirror is possible because of the movement of light rays. Light rays travel from a source, such as the sun, to an object. When they strike an object, they either bounce off or are **absorbed**.

A mirror is any smooth surface that light rays bounce off. Bouncing light rays produce **reflections**. The reflection of light rays produces an image on the surface of a mirror. You can see your reflection in still water. However, if the water is disturbed, the reflection breaks up. This is because the reflected light is scattered in many directions.

Anish Kapoor's *Cloud Gate* sculpture reflects the skyline of Chicago.

How Light Travels

Light makes it possible for us to see. Rays of light travel from a source, such as the sun, to an object. All rays of light travel in a straight line.

HOW DO MIRRORS WORK?

When you look into a mirror, you see a reflection that looks just like you. This is because the surface of a mirror is smooth and shiny. Most mirrors are made using a sheet of glass. The sheet is backed with a thin layer of highly reflective silver or aluminum. However, many smooth, shiny objects reflect images. Have you ever seen yourself reflected in an aluminum toaster, a store window, or a silver spoon? Those shiny objects also reflect. Their surfaces are perfectly smooth. Rough surfaces scatter most of the light, so a perfect reflection is not formed.

Images are reversed in mirrors. That means the left side is on the right, and the right side is on the left. If you part your hair on the right, your mirror image will look as if you part your hair on the left!

Law of Reflection

Light behaves in a **predictable** way. Rays of light travel in straight lines. The law of reflection tells us that light bounces off an object at the same angle at which it hits that object.

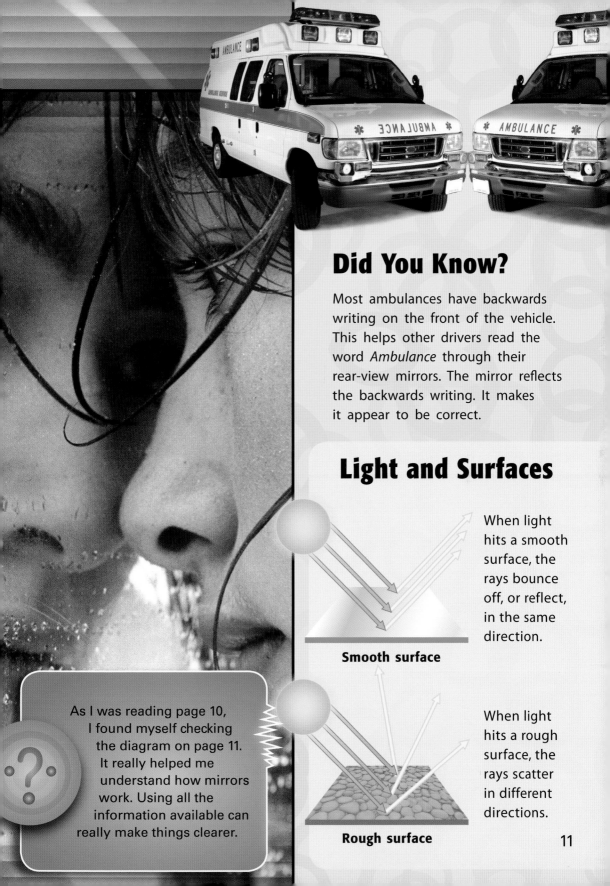

Did You Know?

Most ambulances have backwards writing on the front of the vehicle. This helps other drivers read the word *Ambulance* through their rear-view mirrors. The mirror reflects the backwards writing. It makes it appear to be correct.

Light and Surfaces

When light hits a smooth surface, the rays bounce off, or reflect, in the same direction.

Smooth surface

When light hits a rough surface, the rays scatter in different directions.

Rough surface

As I was reading page 10, I found myself checking the diagram on page 11. It really helped me understand how mirrors work. Using all the information available can really make things clearer.

11

PLANE MIRRORS

There are three common types of mirrors. These are plane mirrors, **convex** mirrors, and **concave** mirrors. The shape of a mirror's surface affects the way in which an image is reflected. Each type of mirror creates a different type of image.

You probably have a plane mirror in your bathroom at home. A plane mirror has a flat surface. It reflects light off an object in a straight line. The image is the same size and shape as the object or person whose image is reflected. That's really helpful when you are trying to see what your face or clothes look like! An image in a plane mirror is known as a **virtual** image. It appears to be coming through the mirror. It is the right way up. But, as with all mirrors, the reflection is reversed with respect to left and right.

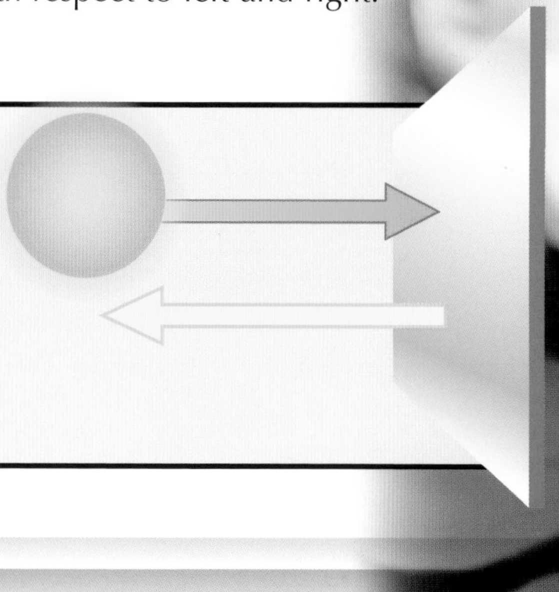

This diagram shows how light hits a plane mirror and reflects.

In Plane Mirrors

- surface is flat
- reflection is same size as object
- image is virtual—"inside" the mirror
- left and right of image are reversed

Main Types of Mirrors

1) Plane mirror: flat surface

2) Convex mirror: outwardly curving surface

3) Concave mirror: inwardly curving surface

Did You Know?

Human babies do not recognize themselves in the mirror until around their second birthday!

CONVEX MIRRORS

Convex mirrors curve outward like a round belly. Convex mirrors are similar to plane mirrors in that an image they reflect is the right way up. However, there are two important differences between the images in plane and convex mirrors.

First, the image in a convex mirror always appears smaller than the actual object. Second, convex mirrors give a wider view than plane mirrors do. This is because of the way in which light is reflected in a convex mirror.

Cars, trucks, and motorcycles have convex mirrors. This is so they can get a wider view of traffic to the side and behind. However, drivers have to be careful. Objects in a convex mirror are closer than they appear to be.

This diagram shows how light rays reflect off a convex mirror.

A convex mirror helps this car driver see that a truck is coming on the right side. Although the truck is closer than it appears to be, the convex mirror has the advantage of giving a wider view of the road.

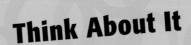

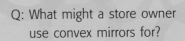

Think About It

Q: What might a store owner use convex mirrors for?

A: Convex mirrors give a wide view. They can help a store owner see customers in the far corners of a store.

15

CONCAVE MIRRORS

Concave mirrors curve inward like a bowl. Reflected light from the inward curves of a concave mirror can produce different kinds of images. The image might be right-side up, or it might be upside down. It might be bigger than the reflected object, or it might be smaller.

A concave mirror reflects light rays inward and then outward. This is because the curve of the mirror causes some light rays to cross each other when they are reflected. The type of image formed by a concave mirror depends on how close or far away the actual object is from the mirror's surface.

Many concave mirrors are used to **magnify** small objects. They make objects that are close to them appear larger. For example, smile into a magnifying bathroom mirror and notice how big your teeth look!

This diagram shows how light rays reflect off a concave mirror.

Both concave and convex mirrors produce images that are **distorted**. Fun-house mirrors have convex and concave parts. They are often wavy. They can make people look much taller and thinner or shorter and wider than they really are!

Think About It

Q: Why might a clothing store use concave mirrors in a dressing room?

A: Concave mirrors can make objects appear smaller. Concave dressing room mirrors might make people look slimmer. This might encourage them to buy the clothes they are trying on.

17

MIRRORS IN HISTORY

Humans have always been interested in their own image. At first, people had to look in still water or at shiny rocks to see their reflections. People began making handheld mirrors thousands of years ago. **Archaeologists** have found mirrors belonging to many ancient civilizations. Ancient mirrors were made of metal, not glass.

People did not begin to make glass mirrors until much later. The first glass mirrors were made in Venice, Italy, during the sixteenth century. Glass mirrors were very expensive at first. They began to be used more widely in homes during the 1700s. By the 1900s, making mirrors had become easier. Mirrors became more affordable.

For many years, the mirror was a symbol of luxury and wealth. Rich women and men had mirrors. Some mirrors were decorated with precious metals, gemstones, and ivory. The mirror probably increased people's interest in makeup, hairstyles, and fashion. People became concerned about how they looked.

Archaeologists have found mirrors, such as this ancient Roman brass mirror, that are thousands of years old.

SHOCKER

According to a tale from the French Revolution, a wealthy French woman made an interesting choice when faced with prison. She was allowed to take only two items with her. What did she take? A pair of slippers and a small mirror!

Numbers used when writing about centuries can be confusing. For example, the sixteenth century is the 1500s. And the 1700s are actually the eighteenth century.

MIRRORS IN ASTRONOMY

Telescopes are tools we use to see objects that are far away. **Astronomers** use powerful telescopes to see deep into space. In 1609, an Italian scientist named Galileo Galilei was the first person to use a telescope to look into space. He used a **refracting** telescope. This was a long, narrow tube with two **lenses** inside. The lenses bent and focused light from planets and stars. In a refracting telescope, one lens collects light. The other lens magnifies the image.

In 1668, English scientist Sir Isaac Newton invented the reflecting telescope. A reflecting telescope uses mirrors to collect light and magnify an image. The Hubble Space Telescope is a huge reflecting telescope. It orbits Earth in space. The world's largest reflecting telescopes are in Hawaii. They are at the Keck Observatory on the **summit** of Mauna Kea. Each of the two identical telescopes at the observatory has 36 mirrors. They form one giant mirror more than 33 feet wide.

Keck II dome

Each Keck Telescope stands eight stories high. It is mounted on a movable base.

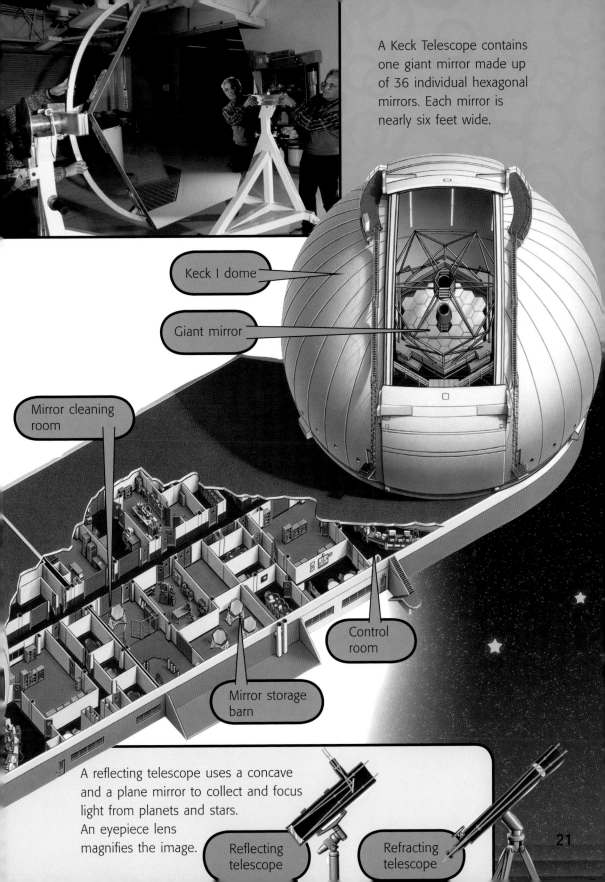

A Keck Telescope contains one giant mirror made up of 36 individual hexagonal mirrors. Each mirror is nearly six feet wide.

Keck I dome

Giant mirror

Mirror cleaning room

Control room

Mirror storage barn

A reflecting telescope uses a concave and a plane mirror to collect and focus light from planets and stars. An eyepiece lens magnifies the image.

Reflecting telescope

Refracting telescope

MIRRORS IN MEDICINE

Microscope

There are many examples of mirrors being used in modern medicine. One example is the concave mirrors used by dentists. Dental mirrors are used to reflect light onto surfaces inside the mouth. They are also used to magnify parts of the mouth. Then dentists can more easily see what they are working on. Medical researchers use microscopes, some of which have mirrors that direct light onto objects. These mirrors make it possible for scientists to see cells up close.

Mirror technology has led to amazing advances in medicine. A fiberscope is a device that uses **fiber optics**. It allows doctors to see inside parts of the body without having to perform surgery. A fiberscope is a **flexible** tube containing thin glass or plastic fibers. A plastic coating around each fiber acts as a mirror, reflecting light around corners when the tube is bent. The fiberscope is inserted into the body. Light is sent through the fibers. The light is reflected off the body part that needs to be seen.

A fiberscope has an eyepiece at one end, and a lens at the other. A receiver sends an image back to the doctor. The doctor views it through the eyepiece. Fiberscopes are often attached to a camera or video recorder.

Dental mirrors help dentists see behind teeth and into the back of the mouth and throat.

dental mirrors

microscopes

Medical Uses for Mirrors

fiberscopes

medical research

MIRRORS FOR LIGHT AND HEAT

Light is the fastest-moving thing in the universe. Light rays travel at an astonishing speed – 186,282 miles per second. That's like traveling more than 23 times around the earth in the blink of an eye! People use mirrors to **project** light to specific places. Car headlights, flashlights, and some lighthouses have mirrors to focus light into a strong beam.

Many sources of light are also sources of heat. Our bodies and many other objects absorb heat. However, shiny objects, such as mirrors, reflect heat just as they reflect light. Mirror technology is used to collect the sun's heat energy with movable panels called heliostats. These panels direct sunlight to a central tower, or receiver. The receiver collects the sun's energy and stores it as heat. The heat is used to make steam, which drives a turbine to create electricity.

Reflective material is used on clothing and street signs for safety and visibility at night. The reflective tape acts as a mirror, reflecting light from oncoming vehicles.

Solar Two is a solar power station in California. 1,926 flat, movable mirrors called heliostats track the sun. They focus the sun's rays on a central tower, called a receiver.

Tower

Heliostat

The prefix *helio-* in the word *heliostat* means "sun." Other words with this prefix include: *heliotrope* – a plant that turns its flowers toward the sun; *heliolater* – a sun worshiper.

MIRRORS IN ART AND DESIGN

Mirrors are not only functional. They can be beautiful as well. The reflection of light in a mirror creates an **illusion** of space and depth. This can make a difference to the feeling inside a room. If you wish to see more of an object, such as a plant, you can position a mirror to reflect it. This may also make the object appear to be larger.

One very famous artist used flat mirrors to review his work from all angles. One might say that Leonardo da Vinci had an unusual fascination with mirrors. He used mirrors in both his art and his science experiments. He created recipes for making mirrors. He drew sketches of mirrors in his notebooks. At times, he even wrote backward, in what is called mirror writing!

A kaleidoscope is a tube with mirrors inside. The mirrors are set at angles. Small items are placed inside the tube. As light enters the tube, the contents reflect off the mirrors.

The Mirrored Room, a sculpture by Lucas Samaras, is mirrored inside and outside with convex and concave mirrors. The sculpture is eight feet by eight feet by ten feet.

Mirrored-glass buildings can be pleasing to look at. They reflect the sky. Mirrored windows also reflect sunlight away from the inside of the building. This helps keep it cooler.

Leonardo da Vinci was fascinated by mirrors:

- he used them in science experiments
- he used them to review his work
- he composed recipes for making mirrors
- he used mirror writing

MIRRORS IN STORIES

Mirrors have held fascination as mysterious objects in stories throughout time. Mirrors have tricked characters in stories, plays, and poems. Mirrors have also told hard truths, such as in some of Shakespeare's works. Mirrors have represented evil and **vanity**, as well as beauty and goodness.

In Greek mythology, Narcissus is so in love with his own reflection that he dies looking at himself! In the tale of *Snow White*, the wicked queen expects her mirror to tell her "who's the fairest of them all." In *Harry Potter and the Sorcerer's Stone*, a mirror shows the thing most wished for, rather than a reflection. And the talking mirror in *Shrek* provides the prince with a preview of pretty princesses.

Mirrors are also used to create illusions for TV, movies, and live shows. Mirrors have been used to create ghostly figures and disappearing people and objects.

Lord Farquaad and the Magic Mirror in *Shrek*

In the story *Through the Looking Glass*, Alice (of *Alice in Wonderland*) uses a mirror to travel to another land.

SHOCKER

Some people believe that breaking a mirror will bring seven years of bad luck! In a shattered mirror, a person's image is broken into pieces.

I couldn't figure out how mirrors could "tell hard truths." As I read on, it all began to make sense. The mirrors don't actually talk, but they do show things as they really are. I guess the author just wanted to say things in a more interesting way.

MIRRORS IN THE FUTURE

Mirror technology continues to bring us new products we may never have dreamed we needed. One company has invented a mirror that can transmit an image to a cell phone or a computer. Another company has created a system of face recognition. It uses a mirror that produces and saves a digital photo. Another company has created a talking-mirror system for security. The message mirror keeps an eye on the house. When it detects anything out of the ordinary, a face appears in the mirror and a human voice reports on possible intruders.

Reflective balloon

Don't Be Fooled!

At first, the message mirror on the wall looks like any ordinary mirror. However, it is part of a home-security system. When the system senses a change in the setting, the message mirror comes to life. A face appears and a voice supplies security information!

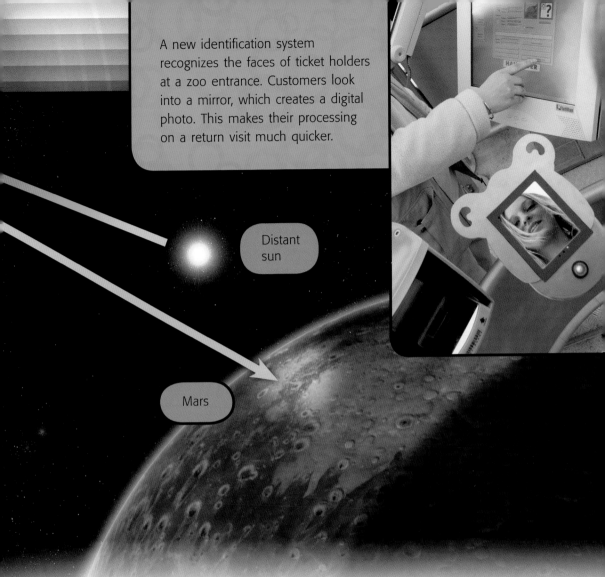

A new identification system recognizes the faces of ticket holders at a zoo entrance. Customers look into a mirror, which creates a digital photo. This makes their processing on a return visit much quicker.

Distant sun

Mars

Scientists at the National Aeronautics and Space Administration (NASA) are studying mirrors. They want to find out whether putting mirrors in orbit could heat a small part of Earth's neighboring planet, Mars. Right now, Mars is too cold for humans to live on. But the theory is that mirrors could act like giant solar panels. They could reflect and direct heat onto an area of Mars. Then astronauts could more easily explore the planet. The orbiting mirror for Mars would be made up of 300 huge, reflective balloons. Together, these balloons would form one giant mirror. The mirror would focus sunlight onto a small patch of the planet's surface.

To many people, space is the last great frontier to be explored. Huge amounts of money are spent on space travel and exploration. For years, people have dreamed of setting up a colony on Mars. Using space mirrors to heat a small area of Mars is one step toward changing Mars so that humans can survive there. But mirrors in space do not come cheap.

WHAT DO YOU THINK?

Should people spend money on space technology and exploration, or should that money be spent on people, wildlife, and the environment here on Earth?

PRO

It's great to know that there are telescopes, satellites, probes, and rovers sending back information about space. People already spend a lot of money trying to fix problems here on Earth. I think it is good to invest in space technology and exploration too.

Some people are willing to invest in technology that will allow humans to live in space. Over the years, as scientists have designed special equipment for space, they have also invented useful materials and technologies for everyday life on Earth. Some people argue, however, that money shouldn't be spent on space technology. There are people, animals, and environments right here on Earth that need help.

CON

People in some parts of the world are dying because they don't have basic things like food, water, and health care. Also, many of Earth's habitats are in trouble. We shouldn't be spending money on technology to explore space. We need to fix the problems on our own planet first.

GLOSSARY

archaeologist (*ar kee OL uh jist*) a scientist who learns about people of the past by studying ancient objects

astronomer (*uh STRON uh muhr*) a scientist who studies celestial bodies, such as planets and stars

fiber optics technology that uses extremely thin glass or plastic tubes to transmit data signals. Fiber-optic technology is used in surgery and for sending telephone signals.

flexible able to bend without breaking

image a physical likeness or representation

lens (*lenz*) a piece of curved glass or plastic in a pair of eyeglasses or in a telescope, microscope, or camera. Lenses bend light rays in different ways.

predictable (*pri DIKT uh buhl*) able to be known about beforehand

project (*pruh JEKT*) to cause an image to appear on a surface

summit (*SUHM it*) the highest point; the top

vanity a feeling of extreme pride in one's appearance

virtual (*VUR choo uhl*) seeming to be real

Summit

FIND OUT MORE

BOOKS

Carruthers, Margaret W. *The Hubble Space Telescope*. Franklin Watts, 2003.

Gardner, Robert. *Experiments With Light and Mirrors*. Enslow Publishers Inc., 1995.

Koscielniak, Bruce. *Looking at Glass Through the Ages*. Houghton Mifflin, 2006.

Stille, Darlene R. *Manipulating Light: Reflection, Refraction, and Absorption*. Compass Point Books, 2006.

Walker, Niki. *Harnessing Power From the Sun*. Crabtree Publishing Company, 2007.

WEB SITES

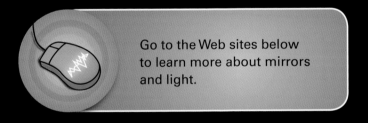

Go to the Web sites below to learn more about mirrors and light.

www.learner.org/teacherslab/science/light/lawslight/funhouse

www.keckobservatory.org/mirror.php

www.fascination-of-light.net/web-lab/kids

www.explainthatstuff.com/fiberoptics.html

www.vision2form.nl/mirror_history.html

http://amazing-space.stsci.edu/resources/explorations/groundup

INDEX

concave mirrors 12–13, 16–17, 21, 22–27

convex mirrors 12–15, 17, 27

dental mirrors 22–23

fiberscopes 22

future 30–33

glass 10, 18, 22, 27

Hubble Space Telescope 20

illusions 7, 17, 26, 28

law of reflection 10

Mars 31–32

microscopes 22

mirror writing 26

plane mirrors 12–14

refraction 20–21

scientists 20, 22, 31, 33

sculptures 9, 27

solar power 24–25

space 20–21, 31–33

stars 16, 20–21

surfaces 9–13, 16, 22, 31

technology 22, 24, 30, 32–33

telescopes 8, 16, 20–21, 32

Venice, Italy 18

Vinci, Leonardo da 26

virtual image 12

ABOUT THE AUTHOR

Laura Layton Strom is the author of many fiction and nonfiction books for children. She has worked as an educational writer, editor, and publisher for more than 20 years. Laura was first fascinated with mirrors when she was a baby looking at her own reflection. Later, her interest was renewed when she read that *Apollo 11* left a mirror on the moon. She also finds it interesting that mirrors are inside many of her favorite gadgets.